NATIVE
AMERICAN
NATIONS

Seminole

F.A. BIRD

CONTENT CONSULTANT: JAKE TIGER

**Checkerboard
Library**

An Imprint of Abdo Publishing
abdobooks.com

ABDOBOOKS.COM

Published by Abdo Publishing, a division of ABDO, PO Box 398166, Minneapolis, Minnesota 55439.
Copyright © 2022 by Abdo Consulting Group, Inc. International copyrights reserved in all countries.
No part of this book may be reproduced in any form without written permission from the publisher.
Checkerboard Library™ is a trademark and logo of Abdo Publishing.

Printed in the United States of America, North Mankato, Minnesota
102021
012022

THIS BOOK CONTAINS
RECYCLED MATERIALS

Design and Production: Mighty Media, Inc.
Editor: Liz Salzmann
Cover Photograph: courtesy of Jake Tiger
Interior Photographs: Ad_hominem/Shutterstock Images, p. 7; AP Images, p. 15; Ernie Hounshell/
    Shutterstock Images, p. 29; Evangelio Gonzalez/Flickr, p. 9; Everett Collection/Shutterstock Images,
    p. 27; fotoguy22/iStockphoto, p. 21; H. Armstrong Roberts/ClassicStock/Getty Images, p. 19;
    Juanmonino/iStockphoto, pp. 23, 25; State Archives of Florida/Guttman, p. 13; State Library and
    Archives of Florida, p. 17; William Silver/Shutterstock Images, p. 5; ZAK BENNETT/Getty Images, p. 11

Library of Congress Control Number: 2021943202

Publisher's Cataloging-in-Publication Data
Names: Bird, F.A., author.
Title: Seminole / by F.A. Bird
Description: Minneapolis, Minnesota : Abdo Publishing, 2022 | Series: Native American nations | Includes
    online resources and index.
Identifiers: ISBN 9781532197222 (lib. bdg.) | ISBN 9781098219352 (ebook)
Subjects: LCSH: Seminole Indians--Juvenile literature. | Indians of North America--Juvenile literature. |
    Indigenous peoples--Social life and customs--Juvenile literature. | Cultural anthropology--Juvenile
    literature.
Classification: DDC 973.0497--dc23

Contents

CHAPTER 1

Homelands

The Seminole Nation is made up of many groups who spoke the Maskoki language. Their original homelands included present-day Georgia, Alabama, South Carolina, Tennessee, Mississippi, and Florida.

As more Europeans colonized these areas, Native American groups such as the Creeks fought to protect their lands. Survivors of these wars went farther south into Florida. They joined Seminole groups who had lived there for thousands of years. Soon, American settlers began calling all Native Americans in Florida Seminoles.

In the mid-1800s, the US government forced many of the Seminole people to move to a **reservation** in Oklahoma. Some Seminole escaped into the Florida swampland. Today, many Seminole remain in Florida.

Many Seminole lived in what is now Everglades National Park.

CHAPTER 2

Society

The Seminole built villages in the **Everglades** on islands **called hammocks.** Hammocks could be reached by canoe only. Hardwood, cypress, and palmetto trees and sawgrass grew on these islands. They also had good soil for planting gardens.

The Seminole built their homes around the island's outer edge. In the center, they built a cook house and an eating house. Guests stayed in the eating house.

The traditional teachings held Seminole society together. These teachings contain the instructions on how to live in harmony with nature.

THE SEMINOLE HOMELANDS

CHAPTER 3

Homes

When the Seminole lived in northern Florida, they built log homes. In the 1800s, the US Army attacked the Seminole. To escape from the troops, the Seminole moved deeper into the swamps.

The land there was soft and wet. This made it hard to build large log houses. So, the Seminole began to build *chickees*. *Chickee* is the Seminole word for house.

Chickees are open-air homes. Usually, they had no walls. A cooling breeze could reach the family from all sides and from below. Thatch covered the *chickee*'s slanted roof.

The Seminole used cypress wood to build *chickees*. The *chickees*' platforms were often built 3 feet (1 m) off the ground. This kept them from flooding during the rainy season. It also kept the people safe from alligators.

At night, the family slept on the *chickee*'s platform. During the day, they stored their bedding in the rafters. Then, they used the platform for everyday living.

CHAPTER 4

Food

The Seminole gardened, hunted, fished, and gathered wild plants. Seminole gardens contained melons, squash, pumpkins, corn, and beans. Their main crop was corn. They boiled the corn and made **hominy**.

The men hunted and trapped. They used bows and arrows and blow guns to hunt game. Men hunted turkey, duck, deer, bear, and alligator. The men also fished in the nearby rivers and swamps.

The women gathered wild fruits, nuts, and greens. They also searched for arrowroot plants. They pounded the arrowroot's stalks into flour.

The Seminole traded with Europeans for food and goods. Later, the Seminole began to farm. They eventually owned cattle and pigs.

All the families in the village shared the cooking house and the eating house.

CHAPTER 5

Clothing

When the Seminole lived north of Florida, they wore deerskin clothes. The men wore leggings and breechcloths. The women wore deerskin skirts. In the winter, men and women wore fur robes. Everyone wore moccasins.

The Seminole who lived in Florida often went barefoot. Women wore skirts made of tree moss or palmetto fronds. Some wore deerskin shirts. Over their shirts, women wore mantles of woven palmetto leaves.

Men and women also wore hats made of woven palmetto leaves or bird feathers. And, they carried bags made of woven palmetto leaves and other grasses.

When European settlers arrived, they set up trading posts. The Seminole gave the settlers animal hides and pelts. It return, they received goods including wool, linen, and calico fabrics to make clothing.

Sometimes, women wore many beaded necklaces. The beads often covered their necks and could weigh almost 15 pounds (7 kg).

CHAPTER 6

Crafts

Seminole men made dugout canoes. Canoes were needed to travel in the **Everglades**. First, the men selected a tall, straight cypress tree. Then, they cut down the tree, sometimes with fire.

The men carved the outside of the log into a canoe shape. Then, they used axes and fire to hollow it out. The men also made **pendants**. To do this, men pounded silver coins into a **crescent** shape.

Seminole women wove baskets and mats. They used cane and palmetto stalks. Baskets stored food. Woven mats were slept on.

In the 1920s, the Seminole began to sell items to tourists. The women made patchwork clothing and dolls.

Dugout canoes could be moved with paddles or long poles.

CHAPTER 7

Family

Clans are important to Seminole society. The clans are named after things in nature. The clans link people and nature to form one big family.

At one time, the Seminole had many clans. But today, only eight clans remain. The eight Seminole clans are the Panther, Wind, Bear, Deer, Bird, Snake, Toad (or Big Town), and Otter. A person cannot marry someone in their own clan. People of the same clan are considered family.

When a couple married, they moved to a new *chickee* within the village. Everyone made sure that the couple was safe and happy.

The village was like one big family. People ate together. At night, the **elders** told stories.

The Seminole are a matrilineal society. This means a child is a member of his or her mother's clan. A clan becomes extinct when the last woman of the clan dies.

CHAPTER 8

Children

Seminole children helped with chores. But there was plenty of time for play. Boys had a few toys. But soon, they learned to use tools and weapons. It was a Seminole **custom** for a boy's uncle to teach him the ways of his people.

Girls learned from their mothers and grandmothers how to tend the gardens, sew, and care for the babies. Young girls often played house. They had dolls made of palmetto and cloth. They made camps of tiny dollhouses and other buildings.

Sometimes, the children had to protect the corn from small animals and birds. This was an important job. Crops were important for survival.

Seminole children learning how to stretch and tan alligator skins

CHAPTER 9

Traditions

One Seminole story tells how the **clans** were created. After the Creator had made Earth, he wanted to create things to live there. He wanted these things to be equal and have special healing abilities.

The panther sat by the Creator's side as he created. The Creator loved to pet his sleek body. By touching the panther, the Creator gave it healing powers. The Creator wanted the panther to be the first to walk on Earth.

The Creator put all his creations, including the panther, in a large shell. He placed it on a mountain next to a young tree. As the tree grew, its roots wrapped around the shell. Finally, the roots cracked the shell. Wind was excited to see the opening. Wind whirled around and helped the panther become the first to walk on Earth.

Soon, the other animals came out of the shell and took their places on Earth. The creator named the animals and put them into clans.

At one time, the panther was nearly extinct in Florida. But today there are several hundred in the wild.

CHAPTER 10

War

Seminole used many types of weapons. Traditional weapons included war clubs, spears, and bows and arrows. Later, the Seminole traded for guns.

In the early 1800s, US general Andrew Jackson and his troops went to Florida. Jackson's goal was to make the Seminole leave Florida and move west to Arkansas.

The soldiers burned Seminole villages. Many Seminole were killed. This began the first of three Seminole Wars that the United States fought. The last war ended in 1858.

A man wears a traditional Seminole warrior costume.

CHAPTER II

Contact with Europeans

In 1513, Spanish explorer Juan Ponce de León arrived on the **peninsula** of present-day Florida. He made contact with many of the native people there. De León also claimed the land for Spain.

In 1539, another Spanish explorer, Hernando de Soto, arrived in Florida. He traveled to present-day Georgia and Alabama in search of gold. De Soto met many Seminole. He tortured and killed them when they did not tell him where to find gold.

The Seminole eventually began trading with Europeans. The Seminole traded deerskins, alligator hides, egret feathers, and dried fish for cloth, coffee, flour, sugar, guns, knives, and brass pots. But the Europeans brought new diseases to the Seminole. The Seminole had no **immunity** to these diseases. Many Seminole died.

Seminole people began to make colorful clothing out of calico and solid-colored cloth from European trading.

CHAPTER 12

Osceola

In the 1830s, the United States tried to force the Native Americans in the southeast to move to Indian Territory in present-day Oklahoma. In 1832, some Seminole signed a treaty that would move them to Indian Territory. Seminole leader Osceola (Asi-yaholo) was against this treaty. He was arrested for refusing to sign it.

Osceola and **medicine man** Abiaka fought against removal during the second Seminole War. Osceola led the Seminole deeper into the **Everglades**. The swamps and hit-and-run warfare helped the Seminole win many battles against the US Army. But Osceola was eventually captured and sent to a South Carolina prison. He died there in 1838.

Osceola was a great Seminole leader. He was born in Georgia in 1804. He and his parents moved to Florida when he was four years old.

CHAPTER 13

The Seminole Today

The Seminole Nation of Oklahoma has its tribal headquarters in Wewoka. This nation has about 12,000 members. The Oklahoma Seminole are descendants of the Seminole who were forced out of Florida during the late 1830s and early 1840s.

The Oklahoma Seminole are working hard to preserve their **culture**. There are programs that teach the Seminole language to Seminole children in public schools.

The Seminole Tribe of Florida has about 3,000 members. The Florida Seminole are descendants of the people who escaped US troops by hiding in the **Everglades**.

The Florida Seminole are also working hard to preserve their culture. They have a website that teaches other people about Seminole culture and history. They also have museums and cultural programs.

Seminole dancers perform at Brighton Reservation in Florida.

Glossary

breechcloth—a piece of cloth, usually worn by men. It wraps between the legs and around the waist.

clan—an extended family sharing a common ancestor.

crescent—shaped like the moon in its first or last quarter.

culture—the customs, arts, and tools of a nation or people at a certain time.

custom—an accepted social habit or behavior of a group.

elder—a person having authority because of age or experience.

Everglades—an area of approximately 2,344 square miles (6,068 sq km) of marsh and swamp in southern Florida. It is home to many alligators, snakes, and other animals.

hominy—kernels of white corn that have been dried and hulled, prepared for eating by being mixed with water and boiled.

immunity—the ability to resist a disease.

mantle—a loose cloak without sleeves.

medicine man—a spiritual leader of a tribe or nation.

palmetto frond—a long, fanlike leaf of the palmetto palm tree.

pendant—a hanging ornament.

peninsula—a piece of land almost surrounded by water.

reservation—a piece of land set aside by the government for Native Americans to live on.

ONLINE RESOURCES

Booklinks
NONFICTION NETWORK
FREE! ONLINE NONFICTION RESOURCES

To learn more about the Seminole, please visit **abdobooklinks.com** or scan this QR code. These links are routinely monitored and updated to provide the most current information available.

Index